# Who's in Charge Here,

**by MORT WALKER**

D1713508

**JOVE BOOKS, NEW YORK**

WHO'S IN CHARGE HERE, BEETLE BAILEY

A Jove Book / published by arrangement with
King Features Syndicate, Inc.

PRINTING HISTORY
Tempo edition published 1982
Published simultaneously in Canada
Jove edition / August 1988

ISNB: 0-515-09776-4

Jove Books are published by The Berkley Publishing Group,
200 Madison Avenue, New York, New York 10016.
The name "JOVE" and the "J" logo
are trademarks belonging to Jove Publications, Inc.

PRINTED IN THE UNITED STATES OF AMERICA

10   9   8   7   6   5   4   3   2   1

6-4

6-27

MORT WALKER

7-26

8-16

EVERY TIME I SEE
THAT RIDICULOUS
DOG IN THAT
RIDICULOUS UNIFORM
I BREAK UP